DESIGNING THE FUTURE

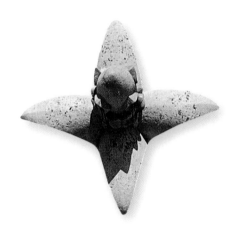

Published by Creative Education
123 South Broad Street, Mankato, Minnesota 56001
Creative Education is an imprint of The Creative Company

Designed by Stephanie Blumenthal
Production Design by Melinda Belter

Photographs by Richard Cummins, Gene Plaisted, Eugene G. Schulz, Ulrich Tutsch

Library of Congress Cataloging-in-Publication Data

Chapman, Lynne F. (Lynne Ferguson)
Cathedrals / by Lynne Ferguson Chapman
p. cm. — (Designing the future)
Includes index
Summary: Examines the history, design, construction, and uses of
cathedrals and describes some notable examples.
ISBN 0-88682-505-9
1. Cathedrals—Juvenile literature. [1. Cathedrals. 2. Civilization,
Medieval.] I. Title. II. Series.
NA4830.C53   1999
726.6—dc21   98-20957

First Edition

2 4 6 8 9 7 5 3 1

CATHEDRALS

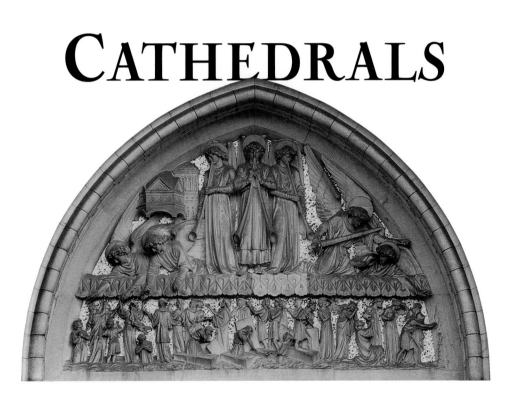

LYNN FERGUSON CHAPMAN

CREATIVE EDUCATION

Father, Forgive. As the old woman stood in front of Coventry Cathedral, reading these words on the wall, she was reminded of the past. She was just a young girl when the Germans bombed this place during World War II. Now a beautiful new cathedral stood beside the charred remains of the old one. The elderly woman bowed her head in understanding. As long as there were people to believe in Him, God would forgive them for their sins.

Ever since the beginnings of the Christian

religion about 2,000 years ago, believers built places where they could gather together and worship. From simple timber-framed churches built a thousand years ago, cathedrals evolved into majestic structures that still dominate the landscapes on which they stand. Even though many centuries have passed since most of the great cathedrals were

France's Strasbourg Cathedral, with its 490-foot (150m) spire (the height of a 45-story building today), remained the tallest building in Europe for hundreds of years until the Eiffel Tower was built in 1889.

built, we still marvel at their massive size, at the beauty of their decoration, and at the fact that they were constructed, miraculously, without the aid of modern machinery.

Cathedrals have always been, first and foremost, monuments to the glory of God. To ensure that He would continue to favor people with

Ely Cathedral in Ely, England

St Canice's Cathedral in Kilkenney Town, Ireland

peace and prosperity, and later award them a place in heaven, His followers wanted to honor Him with the largest, most elaborate, churches they could build.

But there were other, less noble, reasons for building the great cathedrals. During the Middle Ages, western Europe was divided by the Church, as it still is today, into regions, each called a diocese. Each diocese was overseen by a bishop, and a cathedral served as a bishop's headquarters. Many medieval bishops were worldly, ambitious men who wanted to increase their

Aerial view of flying buttresses

prestige. Because these men wanted to build larger, more splendid cathedrals than their neighbors in the next diocese, cathedral building became a competition between towns.

Bishops were not alone in wanting to build cathedrals; ordinary people also believed in the importance of these structures. A cathedral building site could provide work for several generations of craftsmen or laborers in a family. Then, once the cathedral was built, it would continue to serve as a place of learning and inspiration. Beautiful paintings, stonework, stained glass windows, and tapestries depicting scenes from the Bible and stories of the Christian saints provided education to people who couldn't read or write.

Hereford Cathedral in England contains a magnificent "chained" library dating from medieval times. Books were expensive to produce and therefore highly valuable, so they were fastened to the wall with heavy iron chains that made "checking them out" impossible.

Many people gathered at cathedrals, each the center of life in its own community and serving as a place to stage plays and festivals, to produce books and house libraries, to bury the dead, and even to offer sanctuary to the persecuted. Because cathedrals were so important to the towns, people went to incredible lengths to build them strong and beautiful.

One man might envision a glorious new cathedral, but his dream

Pulpit at St. Finbarr's Cathedral, Ireland

Naumburg, Germany

could never become real without the skill of a great many people, including artists who worked in stone, wood, and glass. For these master craftsmen, building a cathedral was the work of a lifetime.

Before assembling a team of craftsmen, the bishop had several important decisions to make. He had to choose a site for the new cathedral, which was often the site of an earlier church that had burned down or simply been outgrown. He had to raise funds,

CELESTIAL

Chartres Cathedral in France boasts perhaps the finest stained glass in the world. The 176 windows, in brilliant shades of red, blue, and violet, include a magnificent example of a rose window.

Speyer Cathedral

Chartres Cathedral's front portal

masons, sculptors, carpenters, blacksmiths, roofers, and glass makers. Each master craftsman was assisted by teams of apprentices, as well as a great number of unskilled laborers. These workers arrived with their families at the cathedral site, where they formed a thriving community.

The architect also had to assemble the materials. The best and longest-lasting building material was stone, and the best stone came from France. Even

largely through gifts of money, land, and other valuables. With the aid of the chapter—the group of clergymen who controlled the church's money—he had to hire an architect, preferably one with an impressive reputation, to oversee the project.

It was the architect's responsibility to hire the craftsmen who would actually build the cathedral from the ground up. These included stonecutters,

S U P E R D O M E

Supported by a hidden inner cone of bricks, the immense dome of St. Pauls' Cathedral in London, designed by the famous architect Christopher Wren, is far more stable than other domes of its kind.

Nave at Belfast City Cathedral, Northern Ireland

cathedrals in distant corners of Europe were built with French stone, despite the fact that the cost of transporting it could be twice as much as the stone itself! Stone quarrying was difficult and dangerous work. Laborers had to chisel off huge blocks from the rock face of a quarry using nothing but picks and axes, then haul them to the surface with simple pulleys and

Detail of a tower on Ely Cathedral

cranes. The quarrymen lived in fear of falling rocks, landslides, and floods.

On the building site the workers laid down the foundation, which had to be very deep to support the massive weight of the building. Then, once the stone arrived from the quarry, the walls could begin to rise. It was a challenge for the architect to design the

Notre Dame stands along the Seine River in Paris

Salisbury Cathedral

walls, pillars, and windows because they not only had to be strong enough to bear the great weight of the roof, but they had to be elegant and decorative too. The patterns for arches and carved pillars were often traced onto a floor, then filled in by the masons, piece by piece, with finished stonework.

Roofing a cathedral was a tricky business. Early cathedral roofs were constructed of timber, but were a fire risk. Later, architects used stone. But stone roofs created a new set of problems, as stone was more expensive to use and more difficult to work with. Each section of the roof had to be hoisted to a great height, and the extra weight of a stone roof sometimes made the walls of the cathedral bulge out.

Architects solved this problem by putting up huge supports called buttresses to help bear the

weight. They also added drainage systems to carry rain-
water away from the walls. Gargoyles, the carved stone
creatures on cathedrals, are actually water spouts that
appear to be spitting on the ground when it rains.

Even after completing the roof, the carpenters
and masons had many tasks left. A decorative vault
went underneath the roof to give worshippers some-
thing beautiful to gaze upon. Often, the crew constructed high towers or spires to go on top of the roof.
Workers could not afford to be afraid of heights,

Bath Cathedral

A Medieval chapel at Ely Cathedral

lead. The effect is beautiful. The great circular windows known as rose windows are among the most striking. French glass makers of the 12th century first designed these windows, probably to represent the petals of a flower unfolding toward the sun. Rose windows transformed the look of cathedrals. The holiest section of the otherwise gloomy interior of the Cathedral of Notre Dame in Paris is brilliantly illuminated by a matching pair of rose windows,

although a number of them, while hundreds of feet up, lost their footing and fell to their deaths.

Stained-glass windows are among the most eye-catching parts of any cathedral. Following a pattern drawn on a table, the artisans had to piece these windows together from hundreds of small bits of colored glass. The glass was first painted and then fired in a furnace. This would melt the paint into the glass. The glass sections were held together by strips of

Detail above the entrance door at Finbarr's Cathedral

Panels of angels in octagonal tower at Ely Cathedral

colored in brilliant shades of purple.

On the inside of the cathedral, workers had to install a strong floor. Some cathedrals had huge circular mazes built into their floors, symbolizing the journey to Christ. Although many of these were later pulled up by church members who believed they were unnecessary distractions, the huge maze at Chartres Cathedral in France still exists, tracing a path more than 650 feet (200 m) long. Woodcarvers, sculptors,

and painters decorated other parts of the cathedral's interior with their works of art, and often monks and nuns offered their skills, embroidering elaborate wall hangings and tapestries.

Though most cathedrals are highly decorated, the design of the buildings often vary. One

A gargoyle

Corridor at Gloucester Cathedral

cathedral has round arches, another pointed; one has a single tower, another has three; one has a vaulted ceiling that's as round as a barrel, another has an elaborate vault crisscrossed with ribs. These are all features of different architectural styles, and in studying them, much can be learned about when and how cathedrals were built. Taking a closer look at these varied buildings, their similarities become evident as well.

Entering at the western end, through a grand

INCLINATION

Pisa, Italy's Romanesque cathedral was built in 55 years, but its 8-story belltower 176 years to complete.

The altar at the cathedral at Cobh Harbour, Ireland

Sacré Coeur Cathedral in Paris

door surrounded by stone carvings, a person encounters the nave, the main body of the church in which people gather to worship. Straight ahead is the transept, running north and south and, like the arms of a cross, dividing the nave from the choir, the part of the cathedral in which the clergy perform the service. Cathedrals are built with this cross-shaped design to remind worshippers of Christ's crucifixion.

An aisle runs along either side of the nave, separated by an arcade, or a series of arches supported by pillars. The walls appear to be divided into three sections. Atop the great arcade on either side there is another smaller section known as the triforium. Above this is the dramatic and beautiful clerestory, a row of

After defeating a town, an angry count lopped off the top of the town's cathedral. Loss of a tower meant loss of face since the tower was regarded as a symbol of power, strength and connection to the almighty.

high stained glass windows which flood the nave with light. Upward further still rests the decorative vaulted ceiling.

A building's relative age can be determined by the style of its ceiling. If the cathedral has a simple rounded vault in the shape of a barrel, heavy, solid pillars, and round arches, it was probably built between the 10th and 12th centuries. This style is called Romanesque, after the Roman style of building from which it evolved.

The twin spires on Cologne Cathedral

Chartres Cathedral

11th-century Spanish cathedral at Santiago de Compostela, with its entrance flanked by two massive towers, is a good example of Romanesque architecture.

In comparison, Gothic cathedrals have a soaring, highly decorated vault, slender pillars, pointed arches, flying buttresses, and a vast amount of stained glass. Gothic cathedrals were built between the 12th or 13th centuries and the 15th century. The designers of these cathedrals aimed for a feeling of great height; when standing inside these buildings, people's eyes are drawn upward to the heavens. A Gothic cathedral such as one in Cologne, Germany, is not only light and elegant, but also amazingly complicated with its intricately carved stonework.

Perhaps a cathedral is neither Romanesque nor Gothic; its designer may have been influenced by other styles of architecture. The architect of St. Mark's in Venice, Italy, who was working during the ninth century, created a Byzantine cathedral. It is highly decorated and richly colored, with five domes similar to the style seen in eastern Mediterranean countries.

Walking into a cathedral, a visitor might sense the countless other people who passed through there over the ages, all part of the building's rich history. At Reims Cathedral, for instance, 26 kings of France

E R O S I O N

The intricate figures on the facade of the Bath Cathedral, show the effects of years of erosion. Many cathedrals fall victim to severe weather.

Westminster Cathedral

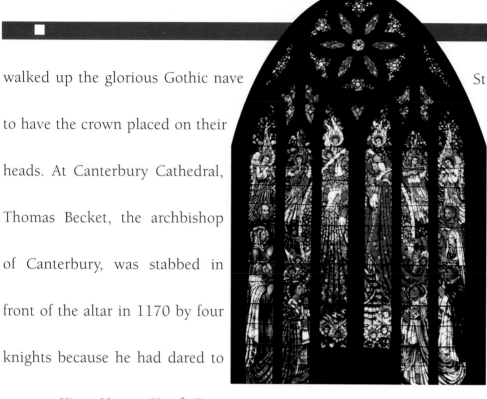

walked up the glorious Gothic nave to have the crown placed on their heads. At Canterbury Cathedral, Thomas Becket, the archbishop of Canterbury, was stabbed in front of the altar in 1170 by four knights because he had dared to oppose King Henry II of England. (Becket was made a saint after his death, and

The Coronation, St. George's Cathedral

St. Thomas's shrine became the most popular pilgrimage site in Europe during the Middle Ages.) Every cathedral has its stories to tell, its own special character and unique history. But all cathedrals share a common purpose for Christians: glorifying God and bringing the Church's message to the people.

DECORATION

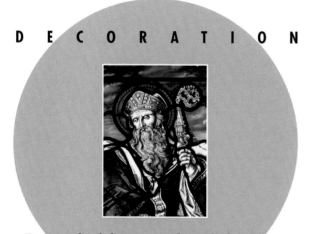

Doors with gilt bronze panels on the baptistry at Florence Cathedral are called the Gates of Paradise.

Cathedrals would be nothing more than beautiful buildings if not for the clergymen who have devoted their lives to serving God and their communities from within the walls of the cathedrals. From the highest bishop to the local priest, each of these people have played an important role in the life of a cathedral. Particularly, men known as monks, and the

Ceiling of nave, St. Finbarr's Cathedral

27

monasteries in which they lived and worked, were often established right alongside cathedrals. Monks often assisted with the upkeep of the cathedrals and other day-to-day activities, but they spent a greater portion of each day in prayer, study, and quiet contemplation. They could not own property and lived sheltered, humble lives.

People living in medieval times must have been grateful to monks for the many services they performed. No poor person was ever turned away from

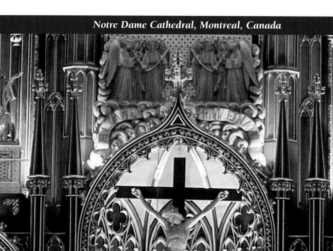

Notre Dame Cathedral, Montreal, Canada

the gates of a monastery. At Norwich Cathedral in England the monks gave away more than 10,000 loaves of bread every year. They nursed the sick, educated the young, and gave pilgrims and other travelers a place to sleep. Monks were also known for the beautiful books they produced. Before the invention of the printing press, they spend hundreds of hours copying, decorating, and binding books by hand.

Not many of these relics remain today. Likewise, over the centuries, many cathedrals have been damaged or destroyed by such tragedies as fire, flood, and war. People who value these buildings have worked to repair, rebuild, or even expand them. Cologne Cathedral in Germany stood for 600 years before 19th-century workmen added a spire that had originally been planned in the Middle Ages.

Today, new cathedrals are still being built. Some traditional styles are still used, but many designs have changed. In the 1960s Liverpool Roman Catholic Cathedral in England was built in a futuristic style from such modern materials as concrete and steel. By

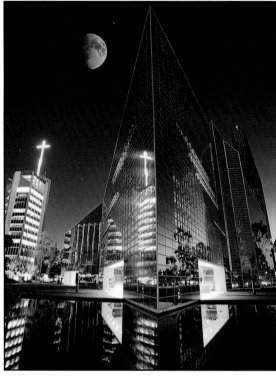

Crystal Cathedral in California

Mormon Temple, San Diego, California

The dome of Florence Cathedral, added by architect Filippo Brunelleschi in the 1400's, took 14 years to complete

contrast, the National Cathedral in Washington, D. C., looks like a traditional medieval cathedral even though it was also built during the 20th century. However, if visitors look closely, they will notice such modern touches as a stained-glass "Space Window" depicting astronauts and spaceships, as well as a gargoyle of Darth Vader!

Even as skyscrapers rise ever higher around them, the great cathedrals will probably stand for many more centuries as monuments to the skill and creativity of human beings and as beacons to those with religious faith. They will remain some of the world's most beautiful buildings, and people's eyes will always be drawn upward to their magnificent soaring spires.

St. Finbarr's, Cork City, Ireland

I N D E X

St. Louis Cathedral, New Orleans, Louisiana